FERRARI
HERITAGE

FERRARI HERITAGE

IN CELEBRATION OF 60 YEARS OF
SCUDERIA FERRARI

RICHARD NEWTON

First published in Great Britain in 1990
by Osprey, a division of Reed Consumer
Books Limited, Michelin House,
81 Fulham Road, London SW3 6RB and
Auckland, Melbourne, Singapore and Toronto.
Revised edition reprinted 1998

© Reed Consumer Books 1990, 1998

ISBN 1 85532 774 0

Editor Colin Burnham
Design Angela Posen

Printed in Hong Kong

For a catalogue of all books published by
Osprey Automotive please write to:

**The Marketing Department,
Osprey Publishing, 1st Floor,
Michelin House, 81 Fulham Road,
London SW3 6RB**

About the Author

Richard Newton is a freelance
photographer whose work has graced
the pages of Car magazine for many
years. His photographic skills have
resulted in many commissions from
major automotive manufacturers for
advertising images. He has recently
been closely involved with Scuderia
Ferrari. He produced the magnificent
photographs in Osprey's acclaimed
Aston Martin Virage. In collaboration
with writer Chris Nixon, this is his
first book in the Osprey Colour
Classics series.

Front cover

The 250 Testa Rossa appeared in 1957,
project chief Carlo Chiti. Chiti smartly
anticipated the change in regulations for
1958 which limited engine capacity for
sports cars to three litres. On 22nd
November 1957, the production version
was launched, with the same
extraordinary cutaway fenders, designed
to cool the huge drum brakes

Back cover

The California drophead was the result
of a direct request from the North
American Ferrari concessionaires in
1957. They wanted a cabriolet based
upon the berlinetta. The California
Spyder went into production May 1958;
the second series, a derivative of the
Berlinetta SWB, appeared at the 1960
Geneva show

Half title page

What is the collective noun for a group
of Ferraris? A paradiso perhaps? Maybe
a fuga precipitosa? This picture was
taken in California, home for so many
Ferraris, both genuine and fake

Title page

Lord Brocket's 250 MM originally left
the factory as a 212 Inter. It was raced
in the gruelling Carrera Panamericana in
1952, crashed, and was subsequently
rebuilt by Ferrari to the later
specifications

CONTENTS

Almost by definition Ferraris should be red, but they also look stunning in yellow

INTRODUCTION

No one book will ever be able to do justice to Ferrari, for there are just too many facets to the marque. For this volume, we decided to look at four of them—restoration, historic racing, collecting and concours. In doing so we have been able to cover a fair cross-section of the marque, which began its life shortly after World War II.

Having been a fairly successful, but by no means brilliant racing driver in the early 1920s, Enzo Ferrari decided that his talents were better suited to management than racing. At the end of the decade he took over the running of the Alfa Romeo Grand Prix team, entering the cars under the banner of Scuderia Ferrari until 1938.

In 1947 he produced the first Ferrari and went racing with it. Ferraris have been racing ever since. Money was scarce in those early days and to help pay for his racing—always Enzo's *raison d'être*—he began to build a few road cars for sale to wealthy customers. Over the years, these Ferraris have been refined from the quasi-racing cars of the early fifties to the sophisticated, Fiat-backed supercars we know today.

The photographs on these pages show only a handful of the models Ferrari has built for road and race track, but they illustrate very well the extraordinary variety and vitality of the marque, which grows stronger and more famous every year, despite the death of its founder in 1988.

In the mid-sixties, Fiat took over a controlling interest in the Ferrari factory and have steadily introduced modern production methods into what was a pretty old-fashioned workshop. There are those who complain that the product has become rather bland as a result, but the fact remains that Ferrari could double its annual production and still sell every car and then some, if it chose to do so. Happily, it does not, because the very name Ferrari is synonymous with exclusivity and the very fact that there is a long waiting list for new cars perversely keeps the orders coming in. It also means that the demand for second-hand Ferraris is considerable and prices are ever escalating, which is why restoration companies are enjoying such a boom period.

Eye-catcher: the Prancing Horse is never far from sight at Monterey

And so is historic racing. Long-established in England and Europe, historics have more recently caught on in a very big way in America and the annual meeting at the Laguna Seca circuit, near Monterey, California, now attracts entrants and enthusiasts from all over the world. Thanks almost entirely to Monterey, dozens of racing Ferraris (and other makes) that found their way to America in the fifties—only to be abandoned a few years later, when they became obsolete—have been re-discovered, restored and are racing again and, in some cases, being shown at some of the very big and prestigious *Concours d'Elegance* in the States. Either way, they also fetch monstrous prices at auction. While this no doubt makes the vendors very happy, it is not such a good thing for enthusiasts, for the extraordinary value of these Ferraris persuades many owners to treat them as an investment, rather than a glorious motor car to be used and enjoyed on road or track. They disappear into very private collections or are just locked away in a secure garage somewhere until the price is right . . .

We would like to thank the following people for their help in producing this book: Bob Houghton of Bob Houghton Engineering; Kevin O'Rourke of Moto Technique; Lord Charles Brocket and Jim Bosisto of the Brocket Hall Collection; Steve Earle and the officials at Monterey, and the owner of the Concours cars, who wishes to remain anonymous.

Chris Nixon

BOB'S 'TOY SHOP'

Bob Houghton began his career with Ferraris when he was sixteen, by stripping down and rebuilding a 250 GT short wheelbase model belonging to a friend. A few years later he joined David Clarke to look after his six Ferraris and this, in turn, led to the formation of Graypaul Motors, where he stayed for about nine years. He was then 'tempted away' from David Clarke by Vic Norman, with whom he formed Rosso Racing in Wiltshire, to cater mainly for racing Ferraris.

Norman is best known as a brilliant aerobatic pilot and once flying began to take up most of his time, he and Houghton disbanded Rosso Racing and Bob decided to take the plunge and go on his own. After starting in his double garage at his home in Cirencester, Bob Houghton Ltd is now housed in a large building at the back of a trading estate in the heart of the Cotswolds, where the business is run in such a low-key fashion that many locals still do not know it is in their village. This is quite deliberate on Bob's part, as security is of paramount importance at a time when the cars he handles are often worth millions of pounds each. Another reason is that he doesn't actually need any more business.

'Over the years we have built up a good clientele and it's all due to word of mouth publicity among the most fastidious Ferrari collectors in the world. We never

At any one time there are likely to be 30 to 35 Ferraris in Bob Houghton's workshop in the Cotswolds, the majority being racing cars. Among those on view here are a twin-cam 275 GTB and a 1964 GTO (foreground). Alongside the latter are two 512 racers, circa 1970, the red one being a special Can Am version which Mario Andretti raced in 1971

The Can Am car's V12 engine was bored out to 6.9 litres to produce around 700 bhp. Bob Houghton received the car from America in several large boxes

advertise and we receive very little publicity, yet the cars never stop coming,' says Bob.

'Clients like the fact that I'm personally involved on the shopfloor, keeping an eye on what is going on. I employ twelve people now and that is enough. I could grow three times as big tomorrow and do all the road cars as well as the racers, but the bigger your company gets, the less you can do yourself and if we were to grow any bigger, I would simply lose touch with our clients. As it is, half the week I'm doing paper work instead of the mechanical work I enjoy so much.'

Despite the phenomenal prices being paid for competition Ferraris, happily many owners are still keen to race them in historic events and the period from January to April is race-car preparation time for Bob Houghton Ltd. Service work comes in around April, after the road cars have had very little use through the winter months and come October it is

Beautifully refurbished, these aluminium brake drums, Boranni wire wheel and rear axle assembly will soon find their way onto a 212 Inter of 1952 vintage

back to the racing cars again. In addition, the engine-build shop is working all year round and there are two men working full-time on restorations.

A man who's work is his hobby, **Bob Houghton** loves to walk into his workshop every morning to be greeted by a floor full of fabulous Ferraris and he likes nothing better than to see others get the same kick from the sight as he does. The one drawback to his job is the fact that some owners don't use their cars. 'We hate preparing cars for guys who won't run them. To spend hours and hours getting a Ferrari into proper working order knowing that it is just going to sit in a showroom or a garage is very depressing.'

Although he looks after mainly racing Ferraris, Bob does not race himself. 'It would have to be a Ferrari and that would be very expensive and anyway, after fifty hours here every week I quite enjoy going home. I have a young family and a life outside of Ferraris, so I like to get away.'

Above
Hero. The very name of the brilliant French-Canadian driver is enough to bring a smile to the faces of Ferrari aficianados everywhere. He died tragically during practice for the 1981 Belgian GP at Zolder

Right
Two more GP cars. Nearest camera is the 1985 Turbo of Stefan Johansson, with Niki Lauda's 312 T of 1973 in the background

Above
*Horizontal Boxer. No, not another
failed British heavyweight, but an
unusual view of a 1976 Grand Prix
engine, the 312 T2. It produced
500 bhp at 12,200 rpm*

Left
*Not that you'd know it from this
photograph, but the 512 M seen here
has revised bodywork, designed to
improve the not-too-wonderful
aerodynamics of the 512 S*

Wall-to-wall 'gasketing' in Bob Houghton's storeroom

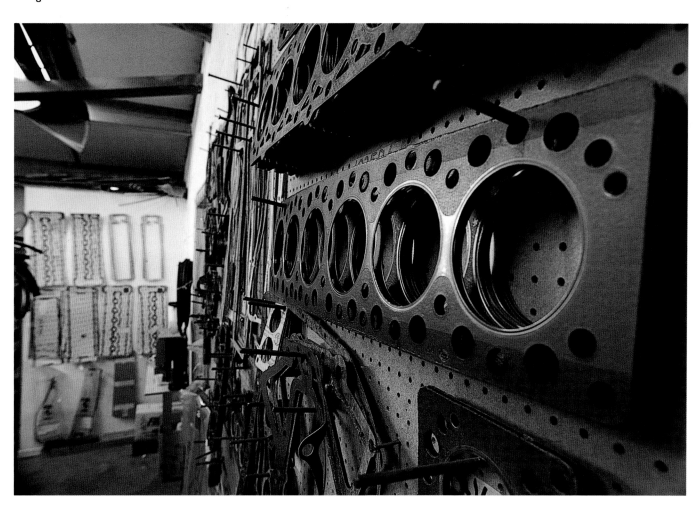

Above
Not prancing, but resting. The Cavallino on this steering wheel boss awaits its 'wheel

Right
Hard-worked racer. This French-owned 1960 short wheelbase 250 GT competes constantly in European historic meetings and looks surprisingly good in its polished, but unpainted state

Above
The distinctive bodywork of the Testa
Rossa was designed and built by Sergio
Scaglietti

Right
This beautiful 1957–58 Testa Rossa
has been totally restored. One of the
most charismatic of all Ferraris, the
'pontoon-style' TR was raced by the
works, mostly with right-hand drive
cars. All customer cars—of which this
is one—had lhd

Bottom end. Looking deep into the heart of a Testa Rossa's 3-litre, V12 engine, which has just been dis-assembled, prior to a re-build. For many enthusiasts, the V12 is the only Ferrari engine. This one produced 300 bhp at 7200 rpm

Instrumentation on the Testa Rossa was, of course, dominated by the rev counter. The TR legend began in 1956 with the two-litre 500TR version, its 190 bhp 4-cylinder unit from engine builder Alberto Massimino. Three World Championships would follow, in 1958, 1960 and 1961. The Testa Rossa signed off in style in 1962, Phil Hill and Olivier Gendelbien winning at Le Mans in a 330 TRI/LM

Left
A 512S emerging from a complete
re-build. Powered by a 5 litre, V12
developing 550 bhp at 8500 rpm, these
cars first appeared in the 1970
Daytona 24-hour race, in which they
failed to finish. They won next time
out, however, at Sebring

Right
A spanner in the works?

MONTEREY MEMORIES

You will always find a dazzling array of Ferraris at Monterey each year, where Steve Earle hosts his Historic Race Meeting every August. Back in the mid-sixties, Earle was a frustrated owner of a GTO, which had cost him all of $6,500. While his native California was the ideal place to keep such a beautiful car free from rust, the roads—with their 55 mph speed limit—were no place to run it. So, when he heard that some like-minded enthusiasts were exercising their racing cars at an airport near San Francisco, he took his GTO along. A good time was had by all and this sowed the seeds in Earle's mind of what was to become one of the greatest historic race meetings in the world. Some ten years later, Steve reached agreement with the owners of the marvellous Laguna Seca circuit at Monterey and in 1974 he organised his first meeting.

Some sixty cars turned up and their races were watched by just under one thousand people—tiny numbers by today's standards, but no matter, the meeting was off and running. To give it a focal point, Earle decided to feature a different marque each year, beginning in 1975 with Alfa Romeo.

'The key to Monterey has always been the restoration of the cars, not the racing or the winning,' he says. 'There was no real restoration industry in America then, and my idea was to encourage people who owned old racing cars but had nowhere to run them to dig them out from under all the junk in the garage and bring them to Monterey. But I insisted that they had to be to their original specification. Originality is the by-word here.'

The trouble with racing is that, inevitably, cars do sometimes get bent and people who own astronomically expensive Ferraris and the like are often reluctant to risk them on the track. They do race them at Monterey, however, for Earle has always imposed a rigid discipline on his competitors, demanding that they treat their precious cars—and those of other competitors—with respect. Invitations to the Historic Race Meeting are hard to come by (over five hundred people apply each year, but only

Previous page, right, far right
*This beautifully restored 121 LM is of
1955 vintage. Scuderia Ferrari raced a
team of these cars that year in the
Mille Miglia, at Le Mans and in the
Swedish Sports Car GP, but without
success. Essentially a 3 litre Monza
engine with two extra cylinders, the
LM's power unit had a capacity of 4.4
litres and produced 360 bhp at
6000 rpm. The cars were very fast
indeed, and Eugenio Castellotti led
both the Mille Miglia and at Le Mans
before having to give best to the
Mercedes of Stirling Moss in the
former and the Jaguar of Mike
Hawthorn and the Mercedes of Juan
Fangio in the latter*

around three hundred are invited) and if you are judged to
have driven in a manner likely to endanger other cars and
drivers you will not be asked back.

Ferrari was Monterey's featured marque in 1984 and
doubtless will be honoured again soon. However, there are
so many competition Ferraris in America that there is
always a marvellous turn-out every year, no matter which
marque is being featured, and there is a profusion of road
cars in the Paddock, too. Whether you like your Ferraris old
or new, Monterey in August is not to be missed.

Right
*Fuel filler and engine air intake for a
250 LM. This model was Enzo Ferrari's
first mid-engined GT car, although at
first the FIA refused to recognise it as
such and made it run with sports cars*

Far right and overleaf
*A fleet of Barchettas. These very pretty
little cars have bodywork by Touring
of Milan and are powered by a 2 litre,
V12 engine giving 140 bhp. Officially
known as the Type 166 MM (the
initials in honour of Clemente
Biondetti's victory in the 1948 Mille
Miglia), they were given the name
'Barchetta', or 'little boat'*

Enzo Ferrari had admired the work of Touring from the very beginning: they had provided the body for his very first creation, the Tipo 815. Then there was a long enforced wait until the post-war 1948 Touring 166 MM. The long-lived design was built upon the Superleggera principle, using sheets of pre-formed aluminium. The 1950 version with 4.1 litres provided 220 bhp

Above
Note the licence plate

Below and right
With its doors open to keep the cockpit cool until it's time to go racing, this 512 S awaits some action at Monterey

Below
The 250 GT Berlinetta SWB (short wheelbase) became an instant classic when it appeared in 1959, with its Pinin Farina-styled bodywork (built by Scaglietti in Modena) and 3 litre, V12 engine. This really was a car you could drive to the circuit, race, and drive home again

Above
The 250 Testa Rossa with 'pontoon style' bodywork is one dramatic-looking sports-racer. Scuderia Ferrari raced these machines in 1957–58 and also built 19 for sale to customers

Overleaf
A 212 Inter—with very low roofline— captured in action

Twisting through Monterey's famous Corkscrew Turn is a 166 MM Barchetta (right), a 1956 2 litre TR 500 (adjacent), a 2.5 litre 625 LM of the same vintage (far right, above), and a pair of 250 GTs (lower right). The 1956 TR 500 was the first Testa Rossa, so called because the cylinder heads on the four-cylinder engine were painted red

Previous page and above
California racing. Regarded by many as one of the most beautiful of all road Ferraris, the California is a drophead version of the 1957, 3 litre Berlinetta styled by Pinin Farina. A few competition versions were produced, with special engines and lightweight, aluminium bodies

Below
*The Ultimate Ferrari. The 250 GTO of
1962–63 is now the most sought-after
Ferrari of all. Only 32 were built, all
survive and when they change hands
many millions of dollars are involved.
Despite their value, some owners are
still happy to race them because that,
after all, is what they are for*

Above
Rear view, and all by Pininfarina. On the right is a Berlinetta Boxer, in the middle a 308 GTS, and on the left a 365 GT 2 plus 2

Above
The 365 GT is a 4.4 litre, four seater which can accommodate four people in comfort

From BB to TR. The Berlinetta Boxer 512 (left) has a 5 litre, flat 12 engine which was carried over (suitably updated) into its successor, the Testa Rossa (right). The latter was named after the illustrious sports-racer of the fifties

Left

Styled very much along the lines of the Daytona was the 365 GTC of 1971. It replaced the 365 GT 2 plus 2, but the rear seats were strictly for small children. The car was not a great success and stayed in production for less than two years

Above

The Daytona was Ferrari's last front-engined two-seater, and the fact that it did not have its engine in the back caused something of a stir when it was first shown to the public at the 1968 Paris Salon. Although rather on the heavy side, its 4.4 litre V12 gave it a top speed of around 170 mph and Pininfarina's smooth bodywork was so good through the air that no unsightly wing of any kind was needed

Left
This is taking adulation a bit far,
surely. Ferrari-worship, as seen in the
paddock at Monterey

Right
Rear view of a rare view. This
drophead Testa Rossa is a very rare
bird indeed. The transparent panels
allow a fine view of the induction
pipes. If you've got it, flaunt it!

Above
*If you can't afford a Ferrari, you might
just be able to afford a Ferrari tee-
shirt!*

Overleaf
*Quatrovalvole. The engine bay of a
308 GTB in its final form, with fuel
injection and 4-valve cylinder head.
The 3 litre V8 produces 240 bhp at
7000 rpm*

'F' FOR FAKE?

Replicars are big business these days. If you so desire you can buy yourself a beautiful reproduction of Jaguar's C-type or D-type models at considerably less cost than the real thing. The same goes for Ferraris, although not long before he died Enzo Ferrari took legal action to prevent people from faking (re-creating?) his models that were out of production—in particular the fabulous GTO of 1962–63.

The GTO and the Testa Rossa pictured here were for sale in California, but neither is the real thing. The former was built by Favré in Switzerland with the replica Scaglietti bodywork fitted to a 1963 GTE chassis. The owner would have liked a genuine GTO (wouldn't we all?), but could not risk running a 10 million-dollar car on the road, so he bought the replica. When photographed, it was for sale at $900,000, but even though it is all—apart from the body—really Ferrari, is it a real Ferrari?

The same goes for the Testa Rossa replica. It looks wonderful, but, once again, all is not what it seems. This machine is a real hybrid based on a 1969 365 GT 2 plus 2 chassis, using a Daytona engine and transaxle. It was built up by a gentleman in Dallas and the sports-racer bodywork was fabricated in Northern California. Although the engine has a red head (painted by the previous owner) the car is no Testa Rossa. Even so, the asking price was $275,000.

So when is a Ferrari not a Ferrari? And when is a Ferrari a fake?

Left and overleaf
It looks like a 1959 Testa Rossa, as raced by the factory that year. The plexiglass air intake reveals twelve carburettor trumpets and the Testas could hardly be more Rossa, but . . .

Left and above
*GTO or GT NO? You can't tell from
these photos, but this is not a genuine
GTO at all. Like the Testa Rossa, it is a
beautifully made replica*

*The real McCoy. An honest-to-God
GTO about to go racing at Monterey*

Above
Did Phil Hill, Tony Brooks and Dan Gurney really race these cars with carpet beneath their feet?

Below
A genuine red-headed V12

LORD BROCKET'S STABLE

Lord Charles Brocket's collection of Ferraris and Maseratis is lovingly housed in the magnificent grounds of his ancestral home, Brocket Hall, some twenty miles north of London, where it is tended by Jim Bosisto and a small team of mechanics. Lord Brocket called upon Bosisto in 1976, when he first thought of starting a Ferrari collection and although Jim has a marked preference for Maseratis he agreed to start looking for 'those other cars'!

Their first acquisition was the 250 GT Cabriolet pictured here, and his Lordship cheerfully admits today that he was not actually fully-funded when he bought the car—getting the cash in the bank before the cheque bounced was a close-run thing! He was, at that time, heavily involved in re-building Brocket Hall and turning it into the magnificent Conference Centre it has now become. In recent years business has boomed at the Hall and the patron has been able to increase his collection considerably without worrying about paying the bills.

Some twenty-four Ferraris are now kept in a purpose-built garage next to a superbly equipped workshop, where Jim Bosisto and his team maintain the cars in magnificent condition, although big restoration jobs are contracted out to specialist firms. Lord Brocket has become an avid Ferrari historian and stores the history of his cars on a computer, updating it constantly as more information becomes available or received information turns out to be incorrect—a not uncommon occurrence, as many Ferraris have very confusing backgrounds. He and Jim Bosisto are always on the lookout for Ferraris and Maseratis to add to the collection, scouring all relevant magazines and attending many auctions.

'But we are not auction buyers, really,' says Jim. 'We'd rather deal with someone who has a car for sale direct, or

250 GT Cabriolet Series Two, looking resplendent at Brocket Hall

someone who knows of a car. We find that most people who are selling a car they have cherished would rather it went to a good collection than be flogged around the country by dealers.'

The Brocket Collection is not open to the public, nor do the cars appear at race meetings or concours events. They are, however, beautifully presented and open to inspection by guests at Brocket Hall and Lord Brocket will also make them available to *bona fide* motoring journalists and film crews upon request.

And, happily, these magnificent cars are not condemned to spend the rest of their lives silent and motionless in their garage. Almost every summer weekend Lord Brocket and Jim Bosisto can be seen and heard giving some of them an airing by blasting around the huge estate or through the country roads nearby. Lord Brocket is not interested in having a static collection and his cars are constantly on the move.

Lord Brocket's Vignale-bodied Ferrari 250 MM of 1953, outside Brocket Hall. This car bears a remarkable resemblance to the 250 S of 1952, one of the most important Ferraris of all which really put the little company on the map with a stunning victory over the factory Mercedes Benz 300SLs in that year's Mille Miglia. The driver was Giovanni Bracco, a private entrant who drove one of the greatest races in the history of the event. The 250 S was subsequently developed into the 250 MM

Above
The 3 litre V12 engine was originally designed by Gioacchino Colombo, who left Ferrari in 1949. It was revamped by his successor, Aurelio Lampredi, and in Mille Miglia form produced 220 bhp

Left
As the fuel tank takes up most of the boot, the spare wheel for the 250 MM is strapped down behind the front seats

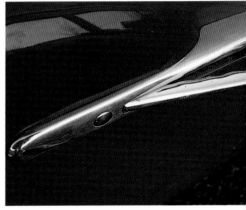

Above and left
Elegant simplicity. The door-pull springs out as soon as the button is pressed and forms part of the aluminium trim-line that runs along the side of the car. The ultra-slim bonnet-stays are drilled for lightness

Right
Wire wheel is a thing of beauty, but the devil to keep clean!

Right
Lord Brocket's car actually began life as a 212 Inter and was bought by a Mexican football star who drove it in the 1952 Carrera Panamericana. He crashed it, sent it back to Ferrari where it was rebuilt to 250 MM spec and given a new chassis number

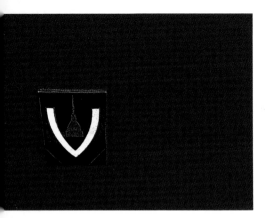

Above
The coachbuilders mark

Right and overleaf
This is a Ferrari 250 Europa GT,
practically identical to a Ferrari 250
Europa. Both have coachwork by Pinin
Farina, but the Europa of 1953–54 had
a 3 litre V12 engine of Lampredi's
design and a ladder-type chassis with
the suffix EU. The Europa GT was
produced in 1954–55 and had a new
chassis which was powered by a
variation of Colombo's 3 litre V12.
Reasonably enough, these chassis
were given the suffix GT and 35 were
built, all with Pinin Farina's Europa
bodywork. Confused? Lord Brocket's
car is chassis number 0421 GT

Above
*Pinin Farina's elegant silhouette for
the Europa GT*

Above
*Lampredi's 3 litre V12 powers the
Europa GT which, as its name
suggests, was aimed at the European
market. Enzo Ferrari knew where the
big money was, however, and for the
US market he dropped a 4.5 litre
engine in this chassis and called it the
375 America*

Left
*Ferrari and Farina have formed one of
the most enduring partnerships
between manufacturer and
coachbuilder*

Below
The interior of the Europa GT

Left and above
Lord Brocket's 250 GT Cabriolet Series
Two which is similar in many ways to
the California, although slightly
heavier. Its 3 litre V12 engine develops
240 bhp, as does that in the long
wheelbase California

Right and overleaf
From the side and front the Cabriolet
can easily be mistaken for a
California, but the latter has a more
steeply-raked windscreen and no
quarter-lights

Above
This 212 Inter of 1951 was styled by Vignale. Jim Bosisto found it on a farm near the Welsh border. The body was hanging from the roof of a barn and the engine and gearbox were in several boxes, but very little was missing. Now beautifully restored, it is almost entirely original

Left and overleaf
*Vignale's use of chrome is interesting.
The strip surrounding the bonnet
extends to the rear of the car and
works very well, visually, but the
bumper is a bit on the heavy side*

Above
Thought to be the earliest Ferrari road car still in existence, this 166 Inter was built in 1949 and registered in 1950. The styling is by Stabilimenti Farina (which later became Pinin Farina and then, around 1960, Pininfarina) and is virtually a copy of that company's superb Cisitalia 202 of 1947, although not nearly so successful in appearance. Lord Brocket and Jim Bosisto discovered the car by accident, in a lock-up in California. Countless mice had made their homes in the original seats, but otherwise the Ferrari was in reasonably good shape

Right
Carlo Boranni is best known for his wire wheels, but the 166 Inter was fitted with his Cabo Sport disc units as original specification

MOTO TECHNIQUE AND FERRARIS 'AT HOME'

Moto Technique used to be housed in a collection of ramshackle buildings not far from London's Heathrow Airport. In and around those buildings were to be found some of the most desirable cars in the world, in pieces. Today, Moto Technique are in far more salubrious surroundings in West Molsey in Surrey, so owner Kevin O'Rourke must have been doing things right. Having started exclusively with Ferraris, the company is now happy to take on the occasional Lambo or Porsche. At the time of writing they have three 275 GTBs, a F1 375, two Daytonas (one a Spyder), two F40s, a good old Testarossa, and a brace of 308 GTBs; (oh, and a Diablo). The obvious question is what are they in for, and the usual answer is 'service', but there is a certain guilty thrill in being told that one of the F40s is at the moment missing its rear and the whole of one side. Moto Technique have now been in business for 17 years, and it is with great pride that the company welcomes back cars serviced in 1981, with very little out of place. Kevin O'Rourke can remember a time when the workshop was stuffed with Dinos – if they disappeared, it would be as if the ravens had left the Tower. Today though, particularly because of the strong pound, there are plenty of different models looking for some tender loving care in the UK.

In contrast, this chapter also includes pictures of Ferraris back at home, at the Ferrari Museum; and some cars that are too new to be in need of the attentions of Mr O'Rourke, just yet.

Awaiting attention at the old and rather endearing Moto Technique workshops are a drophead Daytona, a GTB and in the polythene a Dino

Left and overleaf
Red is the only colour for a racing Ferrari and this GTO (a real one) is having its new finish buffed and polished by expert hands

93

Left
Oops! Hiding in the shadows is the famous ex-Rob Walker 250 GT that Stirling Moss drove to such good effect in 1960 and '61. Stirling was not responsible for the damaged wing . . .

Left and right
There is elegance and speed in every line, every curve, of a GTO. The vent allows hot air from the rear disc brake to escape. Note how the boot lid has been designed around the fuel filler— such style

Right
The 1956 250GT Tour de France was a machine born, indirectly, out of tragedy. After the 1955 Le Mans disaster in which 86 people died, plus Mercedes driver Pierre Levegh, the FIA changed the rules for GT cars. Scaglietti in Modena built nearly all the Tour de France examples, following Pinin Farina's design. The 3-litre engine was the child of Gioachina Columbo, and over time grew from 240 to 260 bhp. It was a road-going berlinetta, but as almost always with the products of Maranello, it was very much a sports car racer, and as such would take fifth overall and first in class in the 1957 Mille Miglia, two victories in the 12 hours of Reims, and three in the Tour de France, 1957-59: hence the name

Below

The 1957 GT Cabriolet (in production from 1960) was rather upstaged by the California Spyder, considered a prettier car. But the lean, straight lines of the Cabriolet have their own charms. The second series, shown at the Paris Salon in 1959, was roomier than the original, with a taller windscreen and quarterlights. The engine had spark plugs on the outside of the cylinder heads which simplified maintenance

Top right

225 Vignale Coupé. The relationship between Ferrari and Carrozzeria Vignale of Turin was a long and fruitful one, from the body for the Mille Miglia-winning 340MM of 1951 to an exotic shooting brake produced in 1968, based on a 330 GT2+2. Giovanni Michelotti was the creative force behind these one-off machines, which were often characterised by air scoops, sometimes with no function, and chrome embellishments

Bottom right

250 GT Berlinetta GB. A fearsome competition car and surely one of the most beautiful bodies ever to grace the road. The racing version would eventually provide 293 bhp with the Testa Rossa engine. Stirling Moss won the 1960 Tourist Trophy in team chief Rob Walker's own Berlinetta, apparently with the radio on at full blast!

Above
Gilles Villeneuve's 1978 T3, with the Boxer engine. Although the flat twelve did not really conform to the requirements of a ground effect F1 car, in 1979 its superb reliability was enough to bring the championship to Jody Schekter

Top right
Alain Prost's 1990 car; who can forget Prost being nerfed off the track at Suzuka at the very first corner by the great Ayrton Senna in his McLaren-Honda? Revenge, in part, for a similar coming together when both were braking for the tight chicane at the same track the preceding year – and that was when they were in the same team!

Bottom right
Gilles Villeneuve's T5, Ferrari's first successful turbo F1 car, at the Ferrari museum. It was in this type that, tragically, Gilles Villeneuve would lose his life, in collision with Jochen Mass

Left and Below

According to John Stanley, in The Stanley Classic Car Yearbook *(Osprey, 1998), 'Ferrari is the third most recognised brand name in the world behind Coke and Rolex; though Harley-Davidson kick up quite a fuss abut these beauty contests ... Ferrari doesn't advertise – owners and admirers are drawn like moths to a candle.' Though the marque cannot help but generate aftermarket 'products', as this shop window in Modena and the Ristorante Cavallino demonstrate*

Opposite

Ferrari 512TR, successor to the Testarossa, went into production in the second half of 1991: 38 more horsepower, 40 kg less weight. Pininfarina stylist Lorenzo Ramaciotti was responsible for the look, including that superbly intergrated spoiler

Below

The F355 Spider; the Berlinetta and GTS versions were unveiled in May 1994. There was a 'problem' with Sergio Pininfarina's latest creation: it lapped the company's Fiorano test track a full three seconds faster than its bigger 512TR brother. Some problem! The last '5' of the designation no longer signified the number of cylinders, but rather the number of valves per cylinder: 8 x 5 = 40. Power steering was available, which maybe caused some mutterings among the diehard Ferraristi

Right

Returning to the classic V12 front engine configuration, the 550 Maranello is faster than its mid-engined 512M predecessor. Thanks to the 5.5-litre engine's 485 bhp, the six-speed gearbox and streamlined underside this remarkably comfortable 1990s flagship reaches 199 mph. Uk cost? Currently about £150,000

CONCOURS VARIETY

The cars featured on these pages are all Concours d'Elegance winners belonging to the same collector. Beautifully restored, they are kept in a centrally-heated garage and only go on the road when the weather is fine. Naturally they are very low-mileage Ferraris.

Many enthusiasts disapprove of the whole 'Concours' ethos, believing that keeping a car in good condition is only right and proper, but keeping it in an artificial state of cleanliness flies in the face of the enjoyment of motoring. Be that as it may, Concours d'Elegance is now very big business, especially in America, where people spend millions of dollars on cars that scarcely ever turn a wheel. You pays your money and you takes your choice...

Considered by many to be Pininfarina's masterpiece, the Berlinetta Lusso of 1963–4 is possessed of a timeless beauty. The rear end incorporated lessons learned on the race tracks with the 250 GTO in 1962, and the elegant little spoiler and Kamm-style tail would be carried over onto the GTB of 1964. Although designed by Pininfarina, all Lussos—350 of them—were built by Scaglietti in Modena

Above
*The 3 litre V12 delivers a modest
250 bhp at 7000 rpm, which endows
the Lusso with a good, but hardly
spectacular performance. Many
owners bemoaned the absence of a
five-speed gearbox*

Below
The inside of the Lusso is not, unfortunately, as clever as the outside. Strictly a two-seater, the car has a tiny boot that is almost filled by the fuel tank and spare wheel. There is some room for luggage, however, behind the seats. The dashboard is a disaster, with the minor instruments in front of the driver, but the speedometer and rev counter are in the middle of the car, far from the driver's eye-line and housed in two huge binnacles

Right
This particular Lusso was originally painted yellow when it was delivered to Maranello Concessionaires. It was purchased by amateur racing driver John Dalton, who kept it for the next twenty-four years, covering only 50,000 miles in that time. Now in Ferrari red, the Lusso has been fully restored and won the Ferrari Owners Club Concours in 1988

Right
A reflection of the perfection sought by
Concours d'Elegance *entrants the*
world over

Previous page and right
*This is a 275 GTB/4, one of the most
sought-after road-going Ferraris of
all. When first shown at the 1964 Paris
Salon (in company with its sister car,
the drophead GTS) the GTB was in
two-cam form and the new models
proved to be the first production
Ferraris equipped with independent
suspension all round, using double
wishbones and coil springs. Two years
later the GTB/4 appeared and the 3.3
litre V12 employed four camshafts,
again for the first time on a production
Ferrari. Another important change
from the two-cam version was the use
of a torque-tube, to encase the drive-
train and reduce vibration*

Left, right and overleaf
The luscious curves of the GTB owe something to those of the GTO. This is another Ferrari Owners Club Concours-winning car

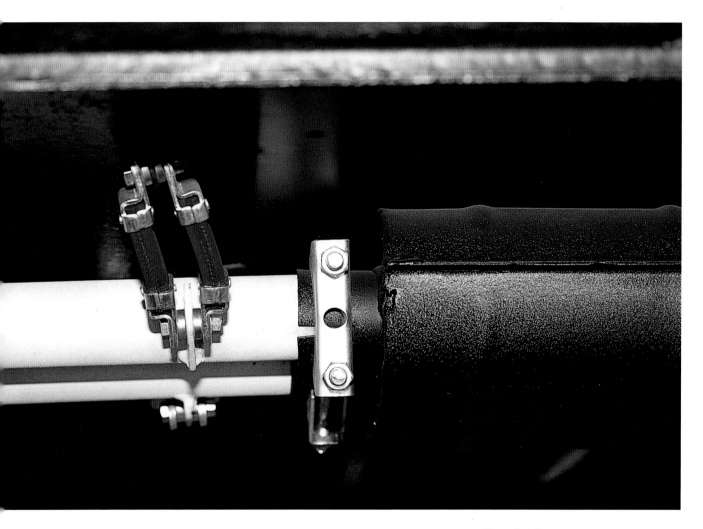

Above

Attention to detail—the exhaust system on the GTB is attached to the chassis via rubber suspension mounts

Overleaf

Sleek beauty. The GTS was designed and built by Pininfarina, whereas the GTB was built by Scaglietti

Above
*The two-cam V12 is the same as that
on the original GTB, but produces
260 bhp to the B's 280*

Below
*Once owned by former World
Champion Alan Jones, this particular
GTS is a rare, 1965, open drive-line
model. Around 200 of these dropheads
were built*

Above and right
Instruments are laid out somewhat better than those on the Lusso, but the interior is strictly for people of the short-legged variety and the handbrake is apparently beyond the reach of the driver when the seat belt is worn!

At some time in the life of this GTS the
slats in the air vents have been
swapped around by mistake. They are
supposed to let air out of the engine
bay, not scoop it in . . .